BOOKS BY DARYL HINE

POETRY

Postscripts   1991
In and Out   1989
Academic Festival Overtures   1985
Selected Poems   1981
Daylight Saving   1978
Resident Alien   1975
Minutes   1968
The Wooden Horse   1965
The Devil's Picture Book   1961
The Carnal and the Crane   1957
Five Poems   1954

FICTION

The Prince of Darkness and Co.   1961

TRAVEL

Polish Subtitles   1962

TRANSLATION

Theocritus: Idylls and Epigrams   1982
The Homeric Hymns AND
The Battle of the Frogs and the Mice   1972

POSTSCRIPTS

POSTSCRIPTS

Poems by Daryl Hine

ALFRED A. KNOPF

New York 1991

THIS IS A BORZOI BOOK
PUBLISHED BY ALFRED A. KNOPF, INC.

Some of the poems appeared originally as follows:

Canadian Literature: *Palinode, Postscript*
Nebula: *The Retreat*
The New Leader: *Côte de Liesse*
Partisan Review: *The First Snowflake*
Poetry: *Window or Wall, Sapphics, Elementary Alchemy*
Shenandoah: *Remarks Not Literature?*
Tamarack Review: *Letting Go, Aubade, In Memory of Christian Ayoub,
     A Small Boy and Others, Withdrawal Symptoms*
Tikkun: *T.E.L., Panta Rhei*
Tri-Quarterly: *Editio Princeps, Woodcuts: au Bois Dormant, Bluebeard's
     Bungalow, Kimono, Tabula Rasa?*
The Yale Review: *Speculations, Et Noctium Phantasmata, Petitio Principii,
     Lucus a Non Lucendo, Unhappy Returns*

Homilies on the Death of David Hill originally appeared in A Catafalque for
     David Hill (Pasdeloup Press)
Alcaics originally appeared in For James Merrill: A Birthday Tribute
Rates of Change originally appeared in A Garland for John Hollander

Library of Congress Cataloging-in-Publication Data

Hine, Daryl.
     Postscripts:poems / Daryl Hine.—1st ed.
          p.   cm.
     "Borzoi book"—T.p. verso.
     ISBN 0-394-58836-3
     I. Title.
PR9199.3.H5P6   1990
811'.54—dc20   90-52946
                                              CIP

Manufactured in the United States of America
First Edition

FOR VIRGIL BURNETT

Ars brevis, vita longa

CONTENTS

POSTSCRIPTS

SPECULATIONS

Another mirror represents,
Askew, a world of difference
Whose optimum experiments
    Are soon surpassed
In retrospect, that commonsense
    Iconoclast.

Broken mirrors still reflect
This fragmentary, strange effect
Like an unlucky idiolect
    Whose parts of speech
Stammer, Only disconnect
    Each from each.

Empty mirrors speculate
Why insignificant and great
Imperfections infiltrate
    The looking-glass
Where unlikeness lies in wait:
    Tout casse, tout passe.

THE FIRST

snowflake that signals
The beginning of the winter
Glistens on the window
Like some early symptom
Of a fatal illness.
Soon the scene is filled with
Whirling white corpuscles
As suicide battalions
Fall on one another,
Building with their bodies
Permafrost foundations
For the icy city
Till the garden's sculptured
Frieze lies under wraps.

Blanketed yet bare the
Trees assume ungainly
Hieratic postures,
Vegetable dummies
Modelling the latest
Thing in winter fashions.
Now prospects that were opened
By defoliation
With the close of Autumn
At once shut up again,
Quaintly claustrophobic,
Like the folded landscape
Painted on a fan.

Pretty as a Xmas
Card, the uninviting,
Uninvited season
Bivouacked outside,
Whether frozen hard and
Fast or snowing solid,

4

Arrests us in its grip,
Prisoners of Winter
Hostage to the weather,
Glad to stay inside
Away from the forbidding,
Beautiful but frigid
Kingdom of the cold.

In those unenlightened
Interstellar spaces
Glimpsed through telescopic
Windows it is winter,
Eternally nocturnal
Temperatures approaching
A kind of all time low.
Even so the silence
There is mitigated
Faintly by a whispered
Microcosmic echo
Like an ancient, distant
Memory of life.

Metaphors are always
False by definition,
Similes too often
Literally true.
Buried in the background
Under all that blasted
Whiteness the remains of
Winter's victims, namely
Our monosyllabic loves,
Pete and Lief and Bud
Cool it in uncertain
Expectation of a
Temporary thaw.

SI MONUMENTUM REQUIRIS*

Cold holds its own inside and out,
More than a mere matter of degrees,
As if zero were an absolute.

Closing the old to open a new route,
Snow drifts mutely through the clear-cut trees
Cold holds, its own inside and out.

A baffled sun is struggling to come out
And celebrate the solar mysteries
As if zero were no absolute.

The frozen earth, as cracked as an old boot
Underneath these frozen fripperies,
Cold, holds its own inside and out,

While Winter, an immaculate mahout
Bestriding a white elephant, decrees
Zero relatively absolute.

Look, should you need a monument, about
You at this classical deep frieze:
Cold holds its own inside and out
As if zero were an absolute.

---

* *Si monumentum requiris circumspice*: "If you seek a monument, look about
you." This boast is still to be seen on many an old edifice.

LETTING GO

I loved you first the time I saw you last,
I knew you best before I let you go.
All the misapprehensions of the past
Dissipated in an hour or so,
Naked to the human eye you lay
Candid as a cadaver on the couch
I could have slept on, but I went away
Ashamed to stay, afraid almost to touch.

Lost, you seemed the only vivid thing
In a world made moribund and flat
By worldliness. Renunciations bring
Their own reward, apparently, like that
Last look of yours, ironical or tender,
A valediction and a benediction,
Which endless reruns will not soon surrender,
The indispensable, improper fiction
Of your unforgettable perfection.

AUBADE

The port of dawn, reluctant to receive your
Freight of dreams, declares them contraband:
What night indulged as everyday behaviour
The *a priori* light of day has banned.

In sleep the disembodied ship was manned
By spooks, the spectres of desire and rancour;
They disappear in sight of morning land
As soon as flimsy fantasy casts anchor.

And yet there is one ghost you cannot lay
To rest among that dissipated band,
Who, unembarrassed by the glare of day
Disembarks on the forbidden strand,

Haunting the banalities of noon
Like a shadow, fascinating and
Unforgiving, beautifully immune
To blandishment, inexorable, bland.

It stands beside you, right at your left hand,
Mute, although in dreams articulate,
A presence that you cannot understand,
An absence you cannot anticipate.

IN MEMORY OF CHRISTIAN AYOUB

Withdrawing from the fellowship of hell
Into some celestial solitude,
You leave behind the noise and heat and smell,
The imps who improvise their torments nude,
For the chilly silence of a place
In which at last you find yourself alone,
Remote from every mortal voice or face,
Including unexpectedly your own.

The Great Low Chamber has no looking-glass,
In fact the furniture is pretty spare,
Consisting altogether of a bed
Of earth where you must be content to pass
Eternity: there are no seconds there,
Not even a second pillow for your head.

ET NOCTIUM PHANTASMATA*

The tacky taste of dreams, my dreams at least,
Simply shocking! Indifferent to *Persuasion*,
    Insensibility prefers to feast
On travesties of Beauty and the Beast
And untranslatable trash, though on occasion
It may engage the dear, disguised deceased
    In animated conversation.

* *Procul recedant somnia* / *Et noctium phantasmata* . . . : "Now let all evil
dreams take flight, / Fantastic visions of the night . . ." Ambrosian hymn
at Compline.

PETITIO PRINCIPII*

Fatal, to put the end before the means,
Similarly futile to regret
Those dinosaurs and obsolete machines
Of pleasure one can never quite forget.

Polymorphous as a Hindu god,
Pain has many faces, arms and legs
Innumerable. Infinitely odd
The unanswerable questions that it begs.

* "Begging the question."

PALINODE

For Will Finley

Orient yourself in time
Toward the prepossessing dawn.
Disenchanted by the past,
Turn your back forever on
The decadent and splendid West
And all your yesterdays in flame.

Tomorrow is a promised land
Inevitable as success
Following the era you
Wasted in the wilderness.
All the prophecies are true
And their fulfillment is at hand.

Tomorrow seemed a sinecure
Available by force or guile.
After your years of servitude
Endured beside the dirty Nile,
What were you able to secure
But exile, want and solitude?

Disorient yourself away
From the disappointing East.
Forget the fair, unfortunate
Fake embellishments of day,
Its phoney promises. The last
Disaster has not happened yet.

PANTA RHEI*

Illusive, the stability of things,
Smoke without which there can be no fire,
Shimmers in the updraft that desire
Creates: material imaginings,
Objects as fragile as relationships,
Irreplaceable at any cost.
Fabric rips, valuables get lost,
And though it has no feelings china chips,
Like people, whom things must not be confused
With, too often smashed to smithereens
Or nobbled in the deadly undertow
Of daily life, off-handedly abused.

But what if all this flim-flam simply means,
Ourselves apart, that nothing moves at all?
            So all commuters know
The disconcerting, transient sensation,
As a train begins to leave the station,
            Of stationary motion,
Refreshment- and shoe-shine-stand, newspaper stall
And platform appearing to slide away, although
In fact the world stands still and still we flow.

* "Everything flows." (Heraclitus)

WINDOW OR WALL

Interruptions in a wall,
Apertures that, large or small,
Serve no earthly use at all
    Save for certain
Openings which seem to call
    For a curtain,

Casements whose transparent skin,
Brittle, paranoidly thin,
Keeps the curious within
    Measly margins,
Framed for looking out not in,
    Crystal virgins

Gazing vacantly toward
False horizons, you afford
Fascination to the bored,
    Plus a promise,
Some exotic, unexplored
    Major premise.

Your integrity, once broken,
Proves to have been only token,
Like a secret that, unspoken,
    Implies it all.
Windows whether closed or open
    Suppose a wall.

SAPPHICS

For Anne Burnett

Usually late, the distinguished season,
Apt to make us wait, seems absurdly early;
Premature, intemperate buds deface the
    Marble of winter.

Green returns, a freshly invented colour
Like a recently rediscovered poem
In a strange but strongly accented metre
    Strictly syllabic;

Time's corrupted text, undeciphered blossoms
Scattered on the grass like discarded garments
Reminiscent of the abandoned body
    That they embarrassed;

Tantalizing glances at tattered stanzas
Fragmentary as an archaic statue
Damaged by the passage of feet and ruined
    By restoration,

Legible as longing, a romance language
Conjugated annually with liquid
Consonants, irregular endings, florid
    Vigorous verb-stems:

*Night ... and maidens ... singers ... nocturnal friendship
(Love?) ... a nymph with violet breasts ...* These doubtful
Readings satisfy our indecent human
    Weakness for meaning,

Which appears no easy illusion. Each
Lacuna punctuating the fragrant fragments
Written in the spring of the world translates a
    Grammar of silence.

EDITIO PRINCEPS*

Austere and unforgiving spring
    Overshadowed by malaise,
    Precocious, tantalizing days
Protracted into evening
    By the sun's reluctant rays,

Everything you touch awakes
    Unenthusiastically,
    Such as this stark, naked tree
That, awkward and unsightly, breaks
    Out in the throes of puberty,

Or these modest, backward flowers,
    Inhibited by circumstance,
    The genitalia of plants,
More delicately fleshed than ours
    In their coloured underpants.

With seasonable tardiness
    As subscribers we enjoy
    On the doorstep or nearby
Two leavings of the daily press
    Each flung by a different paper boy:

First the surreptitious one,
    Unencouraging and cold,
    Then, open as a centrefold,
His buddy, in comparison
    Forward, foul-mouthed, fresh and bold.

The lad who brought *The Morning Star*,
    Shy and silent with the dawn
    Unobserved has come and gone,
Unlike the more spectacular
    Youth who brings *The Evening Sun*.

* First or principal edition.

16

LUCUS A NON LUCENDO*

Inexorably a praying mantis swings
Back and forth its ruthless wrecking ball.
Too close for comfort, *Quiet Hospital
Zone* signals pandemonium. As things
    Stand or, rather, fall,
The only quiet here is terminal.
Next door the What's-Its-Name Memorial
    Convalescent Wing's
A grove that neither grows nor glows at all.

Some other paradoxes that we call
Misnomers: Catholic intellectual,
English muffins, Labour Day, adult
Entertainment, and that popular
Poppycock mislabelled The Occult.
Masterpiece Theatre might soon decrease
Its ratings if it risked a masterpiece.
    How interchangeable are
Those sentimental favourites, war and peace!

---

* Literally, "A grove, so-called from not glowing." Hence, any punning paradoxical definition or derivation.

CÔTE DE LIESSE

For David Tacium

My disaffected gaze falls on the city
Of my youth, what's left of it. It winks
Back with insomniac, hypnotic eyes
Which sunrise is beginning to surprise.
Distinct, but less distinguished than it thinks,
The sleepy urban university

Where I matriculated twenty odd
Years ago, seen from this twenty-third
Floor has altered out of recognition,
As if a revolution had occurred
Without my knowledge in the intermission
Between the acts—perhaps an act of god?

A handful of pedestrians like pigeons
Flutters across the pavement, obsolescent
Not only because they hunt and peck on foot,
But as the scattered relics of religion's
Locally outmoded, adolescent
Habits as impeccable as soot.

Light filters into focus, fills my field
Of vision till I long to turn away,
Discomfited by dawn's proximity.
At last the night that napkined up the day
Unfolds, and Royal Mountain is revealed
Ridiculous in its sublimity,

A pimple on the spotty, pock-marked plain
That stretches, interrupted by the river,
Cluttered by indifferent slum clearance
And building blocks, apparently forever . . .
The past is nothing but a disappearance
The present is unable to explain,

Little of either visible to my
Myopic, lackadaisical researches
Into the afterlife of Montreal,
At the rate that cities live and die,
Changed beyond recall. So are we all.
Bells keep tinkling in the empty churches.

UNHAPPY RETURNS

With all the sinister abruptness of
Involuntary memory in Proust
Imaginary flights return to roost.
Sudden and insidious as love,

The telephone's coercive, tinny laugh
Interrupts, and thus defines, an idyll,
Peremptory, inserting in the middle
Of a meal, a nap, a paragraph

Word of a law-suit or a legacy,
Congratulations, gossip and complaint,
And yesterday a minatory, faint
Voice, "It's Nemesis. Remember me?"

NORTHWEST PASSAGES

Here low tide and morning coincide
When ocean's underside, as if a veil
Were twitched aside, denuded by the tide,
Emerges flat, unprofitable, stale.
Here pubescent forests fail to hide
The five-o'clock shadow on the mountainside
Close shaven to make newsprint and junk mail.
Here civilization, predominantly male,
Perpetrates unnatural matricide.

Snooty, aloof, polluted mountaintops,
Stuck-up, their heads forever in the clouds
While they cold-shoulder low-brow tourist traps
Strike forbidding, lofty attitudes
Against a breathless sky, sublimely iced.
How isolated and exclusive are
These uninhabitable altitudes
Domesticated by the calendar,
The picturesque prohibitively priced.

Stark on the covers of slick magazines
Where landscapes look too beautiful for words
The wilderness excels at making scenes.
Its present rate of defloration means
That travel nowadays is for the birds.
The home of mobile homes away from home,
Once the haunt of cormorants and cranes,
Of eagle and of seagull, has become
The realm of Burger Kings and Dairy Queens.

WOODCUTS: AU BOIS DORMANT

For Doug Wilson

There are worse materials than wood.
Iron rusts and stone resists, so hard
That, once manhandled, marble may be marred
Forever. Glass is fragile, plastic good
For nothing much but junk. They understood
This matter as a medium who scarred
Whole forests carving totem poles that stood
Where I come from in everyman's back yard.

Woods which were enchanted after dark
Once upon a time, the haunt of creeps
Reputedly, today are lumbered with
The rigid regulations of a park.
Nonetheless the past returns as myth:
In fairy tales it is the wood that sleeps.

SEQUESTERED IN THE DARK GARAGE

Sequestered in the dark garage
I listened to the broken voices,
Suspiciously well-spoken, vicious,
Reiterate erotic garbage.
How few, how far from infinite
The constellations of their vices
Filled that artificial night
Where synthetic innocence
Initiated the debauch
Of the dubiously butch.
Nor have I forgotten since
The hardware that below their belts
In the bath-house at the beach
The crude compared to nuts and bolts.

This was the seductive scene
Of those first experiments
Tantamount to sacraments,
Involving a comparison,
Competitive and curious,
Between each others' various
Degrees, durations, and amounts:
Invidious undress parade.
For every member that obeys
The laws of nature, some abuse
The privilege, priapic, proud.
An ecstasy they cannot sham
Announces puberty to boys,
But girls mature in bloody shame.

A SMALL BOY AND OTHERS

Perched upon a pedestal, he saw
Perfection in an adolescent; then,
Dissatisfied with what he could not draw,
Put down the pencil and picked up his pen.

Is this the image he feared to enjoy
Openly in exile, while he penned
So many portraits, none of that dead boy
Whose likeness he kept by him to the end?

Perhaps the secret of a style oblique
Enough for anything, including truth,
Appears in the ingenuous physique
Of a devoted, unselfconscious youth.

Divested of every garment, he beheld
'Life' on a pedestal and in a pose
Cheerfully immodest, which it held
While he essayed to capture it in prose.

And if he never really got it right,
Anyway the old pretender tried
To keep the lifelike now and then in sight.
The master havered till the model died.

THE IDYLLS OF THE BARON

Perfectly straight-faced, a little wooden,
Provocatively semi-soft, they sprawl
Against the cardboard rocks and waterfall
Of gauze, in antique photographs von Gloeden
Took of their hardy, common, commonplace
Bodies embellished by the classic work
Of shepherd, chauffeur, shop-boy, shipping-clerk
With a banal, anachronistic grace.

All of them are dead today, of course,
Dead as Daphnis, all the evidence
Of their beauty these anomalous
Images that crudely reinforce,
Conjugated in the perfect tense,
A misconception of Theocritus.

T. E. L.

To lighten his sad eyes you did it all.
The freedom you had wrought in Eros' name,
(Hearing he had died before you came
Through silken dust to see Damascus fall),
You threw away, until *there should remain
Not anywhere now rest and peace at all*
Unless in self-denial, secret, small
Acts of kindness, penitence, and pain.

The saints' besetting sin is being wrong,
And their redeeming grace, it does not matter
That what they worshipped was not really there.
You erred about the Arabs and the air;
The former proved ungrateful, and the latter
An element where men do not belong.

GENESIS

As told to whom? redundant lives
Epitomize just how absurd
Pseudonymous attributions are.
A name commemorates a word
In which significance survives
Solely in the singular.

The prime ghost-written text, the Bible,
Libelled by creationists
As a literal translation
Betrays its authorship in scribal
Errors for whose interpretation
No original exists.

REMARKS NOT LITERATURE?

For Michael Sweet and Leonard Zwilling

History blackballed
A nation of sorts whose past
    Is present and which
Knew no Reformation
Renaissance or Enlightenment,

    Only incessant
Revolution, a macho
    Burlesque that proclaims
Ugliness a solution
For the poor and picturesque.

    Even the bloody
Pyramids are pointless. What
    To do with the wheel
Stumped those whose countless rebuilt
Ruins still ruin the view.

    Once they invented
The step they just couldn't stop,
    Dotting the desert
With trapezoid, indented
Structures with nothing on top.

    These neolithic
Nouveaux riches idolized blood
    Shed and cosmic greed,
As shown in hieroglyphic
Codices no one can read.

    Cannibalism
Was less an end than a means:
    Ecologically
No other organism
Provided enough proteins.

Noble savages
After all, as a rule they
        Sacrificed their neighbours,
But playing ritual
Hard-ball the winners got iced.

An unstable table
Land settled by successive
        Tribes each nastier
Than the last can barely
Support its excessive past.

One feels a sneaking
Brotherhood with that friar
        Who for the natives'
Eternal good suppressed their
Perpetual calendar.

A fad for the fake
Primitive still seduces
        Sophisticated
Savages into making
Junk they do not use to live.

Half-baked, misshapen
Imperfectly watertight
        Jugs affect to be
Unearthed stratigraphically,
Museums of ugly mugs

Whose wretched design
And workmanship label a
        Thing as handmade. The
Ubiquitous microchip
Has boosted the tourist trade.

Precolumbian,
Prosaic, yet frightfully
    Strict, syllabic bits
Of the crazy mosaic
Reflect more than they depict.

Metrically far-fetched,
These rhymes of a stay-at-home
    May nevertheless bring
Back those prehistoric times
On and off the beaten track.

Not always so well
Expressed, fellow-travellers'
    Obiter dicta
Should interest those who think
Remarks are literature.

THE RETREAT

For Sam Todes

Home again at last! the weeks away
Worse than wasted, for the world is not
After all a pleasant place to stay:
Half supermarket and half parking-lot.

With cities, once the playground of the young,
In ruins, now urbanity has failed,
Civil senior citizens belong
Here in this domesticated, wild

Amalgam of downtown and countryside,
A civilized yet rustic compromise
Where Indolence and Industry reside
In a synthetic, tidy paradise.

The silence of suburban afternoons
Reverberates with din that interrupts
Insistent crickets shrill as telephones;
Power mowers show how power corrupts.

A prepubescent lawn, too young to shave,
Overshadowed by a grown-up hedge,
Embellishes the geriatric grove,
And evergreen, rococo foliage,

Through which reticulated screen, unseen
But sensible, a breeze insinuates
That somewhere out of sight behind the scene
Summer's cold-blooded understudy waits.

RIDDLE

Invisible, chimerical
Revolution of the air,
Fickle, hyperactive, fair,
Impulsive, unpredictable
Flibbertigibbet capable
Of never settling anywhere;
Fortuitously musical
Condition of the atmosphere,
Zephyr, monsoon, hurricane,
Tempest, typhoon, gust or gale—
When will inspiration fail?—
Accomplice of the hail and rain,
Blind but palpable as braille

Wind animates the weathervane.

WINDFALL

The storm that roused us after midnight left
A brash intruder peering in our window.
Thunder grumbled, hectic lightning laughed
As rain was worried frantic by the wind. A
Sentinel adopted as a perch
By every kind of flighty riff-raff crashed
Overnight dead broke on our back porch
Where it welcomes me this morning, smashed
As an unexpected, tipsy guest
Who asks no invitation to drop by,
Or like a green, decapitated ghost
Breezily descended from the sky.

BLUEBEARD'S BUNGALOW

Beneath the living room, inside the crawl
Space, in makeshift graves at most skin-deep,
Beauties whom the beast abandoned sprawl
Awkward, anonymous, as if asleep
Till at the resurrection flesh will creep
And, while all earthly memories are rotten,
Their fake identities will be forgotten.

Uncounted throwaways, their cocksure, carnal
Natures, convinced the devil couldn't care
Less, betrayed them blameless to this charnel
House to be garotted with a prayer.
A spare room holds a magazine of spare
Parts; discarded in the attic lies
The latest broken plaything. Otherwise

Superficially immaculate,
The shambles masquerades as Shangri-la,
Where many an immature unfortunate
Was guaranteed from growing older, a
Terminal but fashionable spa
Any mass-murderer might be at home in,
Since Bide-a-Wee is next door to Dun Roamin.

As on a grander stage a darker age's
Magnificent original Blue Beard
Haunts legend's ill-illuminated pages,
Satan stalks suburbia, less feared
Than frowned on; wickedness winked at as weird
Profaned with sinister experiments
The Chapel of the Holy Innocents.

Cheaper than tears and easier to shed,
Blood percolated in the songbird's throat,
All for another pretty severed head
Or ultimate, excruciating note,
But Justice blackly capped that heartless quote,
("Once the voice is broken, break the neck.") :
"Vous vous tourmentez et moy avecques". *

* Words of the judge at the trial of Gilles de Rais (1404–1440).

WITHDRAWAL SYMPTOMS

The apathetic landscape swallows
    Up its features one by one,
Grey eminences, sleepy hollows,
    Fading with the setting sun,
Fall into the dark that follows
    Like a shadow everyone.

Dazzled by day's bright example,
    Nights in sullen Autumn grow
Unambiguously ample,
    Boring, middle-aged and slow
As the heavy hours that trample
    On insomniac tip-toe.

Life's perimeter keeps shrinking
    By degrees, not opening
Up, unlike the rude, unthinking,
    Exhibitionistic Spring,
Nature's vital fluids sinking
    Underground in everything.

Victims of seasonal harassment,
    Wracked romantic trees perform
Agonies of self-effacement
    Stripped and stricken by the storm;
Meanwhile huddled in some basement
    Life is trying to keep warm.

HOMILIES ON THE DEATH OF
DAVID HILL, PAINTER (1914–1976)

Of all the deaths of Autumn, his alone
Touches us at less than one remove.
While the demise of strangers better-known
Can leave us cold, an intimate's may prove
An object lesson in how not to live.
His failure, for which time may yet atone,
Reproves success, for nothing can postpone
Posterity's sly interrogative.

Yet this fastidious and candid hand,
Rarely failing to beguile the eye,
Unfashionable, fashioned in the end
More than enough to be distinguished by,
As much as anyone will leave behind,
An evidently natural *trompe l'oeil.*

Still lives distill a static, cluttered, staid
Stale life, the bric-à-brac of circumstance;
Chiaroscuro adumbrates a shade
Of understatement, every nuance
That overclouds these shady landscapes like
Shadows of tenebrous experience;
Unflattering, each likeness represents
The virtual transcendence of technique.
Architectural perspectives feel
Infinite, until they end in green
Imaginary gardens with unreal
Denizens whose stylized libertine
Antics anticipate in no detail
A present reprehended as obscene.

In the corny allegory, Art
Versus Life, perhaps he had no more
Than an honourable walk-on part,
But none excelled his patient penchant for
Perfection, which must be its own reward,
Now that excellence is out of date
In an imperfect world which can afford
Only the ephemeral fifth-rate.

A martyr, which is not to say a saint,
And anything but an iconoclast,
The hardships he enjoyed defied complaint.
So he came to exemplify at last
Past masters who had taught him how to paint
In an age oblivious of the past.

KIMONO

Sloppy oriental sleeves
Accidentally enough
Sweep the board and dabble in the sink.
The tree of which these are the leaves,
Woven of some rough, druidic stuff,
Is rooted deeper than you think
In what flesh naturally believes.

Animal fabrics, silk and wool
Do not wrinkle, like the fur
With which some beastly creatures are endowed.
Falling to my feet in full
Folds, this habit I prefer
To wear to shreds enwraps me like a shroud,
Custom-tailoured, comfortable.

SUTTEE

For Marya Fiamengo

What loomed a lyrical ascent
    Looks downhill all the way,
To deconstruct that decadent,
    Ambiguous cliché:
The same declivity that meant
    Ease signifies decay,
When savings not already spent
    Are daily cast away.

The less to eat, the less to drink,
    The worse a cigarette
Tastes. But one sense doesn't shrink,
    The sense of vain regret
For errors entered in red ink
    Indelibly marked *stet.*
A blinking lighthouse on the blink,
    Can memory forget?

Of ruined appetites, the last
    Is impotent desire
Which wishfully rewrites the past
    Then feeds it to the fire
In a reluctant holocaust
    In principle entire,
Like those devoted widows caste,
    Not grief, prods to the pyre.

ALCAICS

For James Merrill

No worse than last year, better than years to come,
Life may afford a metrical breathing space
      Like fixed caesuras in classic
        Alexandrines or in Anglo-Saxon

Alliteration. Time doesn't always rhyme,
But fidgets, limps, tip-toes on uneven feet,
      Each stress a syncopated heart-beat
        Rising and falling in lyric accents.

How many measured syllables will it take
To shape the end-stopped strophes of sixty odd
      Lines scanned as rhythmic prose or free verse,
        Marked by increasingly rare enjambments?

Though meaning may be marginal anyway,
Still here in handpicked words is the long and short
      Of it: revise old age's strict blank
        Verse in a series of spiffy stanzas.

ELEMENTARY ALCHEMY

Vivid season of decay,
Deliquescent as a dream,
Was it only yesterday
That those fugitives which seem
So perspicuous today
Grew impenetrably green
Against an unencumbered sky?
So our brittle lives have been
Worse than decimated by
Time's unstoppable machine
By gravity condemned to fly.

Matter, our material,
Should not matter, but it does,
Alas! And everything that was
Once light and insubstantial
Suddenly solidifies,
The world, so gross, so wonderful,
Becoming right before our eyes
Opaque and permanent and dull
As the fulfillment of a wish,
Which metamorphoses recall
The limitations of the flesh.

Seasons, every way they turn,
Remind us of their precedents;
Each leaf unseasonably torn
From the text of life presents,
Illegible and taciturn,
Tainted, tarnished evidence
Of our future decadence
Which we are bright enough to burn.
Illuminated documents
As if by alchemy return
To their old-fashioned elements,

Of which tradition taught that there
Were four, though some imagined one.
Water is the Spring's affair,
Whether it will stand or run;
Earth, a spin-off of the sun,
Grows exuberantly fair
Under Summer's benison;
Winter, Fall's apparent heir,
Once the patient has begun
To die, adopts a frigid air
Of mourning till the year is done.

Fire that purrs, feline and furry,
Domesticated in the stove,
Freed becomes a frantic fury.
Whole autos-da-fé of love,
Adept in which refining, fiery
Furnace ardent martyrs move,
Blaze in an autumnal grove,
Colours kindled by the fairy
Gold and conflagration of
Fall, whose tragic, transistory
Riches Winter will remove.

RATES OF CHANGE

Summer's consolation, leaves,
Some emblematic, lose their grip;
North to South one soon perceives
A disparate relationship.

Across the border, tropes that burned
Trite, a transformation scene,
Like the currency have turned
A uniform, devalued green.

TABULA RASA?*

For John Hollander

Titivate: cosmetic task
like cleaning up   a cluttered desk
to disinter   a dud decade
too undecided   to decode.

Drifted drafts   of dry leaves make
decomposition   run amuck:
iffy *if*s   and *but*s and *and*s,
abandoned means   aborted ends.
Legible leftover   language litters
the blankety-blank   embarrassed blotter's
doodles, indelible   dead letters
dictated but   not signed indeed
by the effete   influential dead
whose symptoms I   cannot deny:
Tennyson's elbow   Housman's knee.

Tabula rasa: trash the past?
scrap these screwed-up   scribbled post
scripts, pathetic   unpaid bills,
parodies   or parables?
Beg the question   and begin
anew and ever   more again,
ex nihilo?   perhaps not quite
now every *bon mot*   is a quote.
For plagiarists   and staircase wits
taste's wastebasket   always waits.

* "A clean slate."

45

POSTSCRIPT

I wrote the world and its reply
Arrives in this white envelope,
Inevitably self-addressed
And stamped with its own worldliness,
Bleak season's greetings tendered by
A winter who could hope to cope
With coolly? Nothing but the best
Wishes of the wilderness.
Beyond a horizontal plain
Sealed by the incessant snow,
A table that has raised itself
Immaculate of vital stain,
Ornamental fir-trees grow
Like bibelots upon a shelf.

Morning's metrical plateau
Erodes to desert afternoon,
The waste of time, with one oasis,
Comfortable evening,
Nocturnal bottomlands where flow
The frozen rivers of the moon
Through unilluminated places.
Virtually everything
Caught in earth's magnetic field,
Mountains, forests, valleys, seas,
With their obscure inhabitants
Is in time compelled to yield
To the rhythm that decrees
The patterns of diurnal dance.

Day and night and night and day
Never cease to alternate
Like the flickers on a screen
That represent reality.
Tentatively twilight's grey,

Spectral, indeterminate
Status hesitates between
Brilliance and obscurity.
Day is masculine in most
Languages, night feminine;
As opposites they interact.
Twilight as befits a ghost
Seems neuter. Day and night begin
To differ in the entr'acte.

As the climax of a piece
Divided into three or five
Acts and twice as many scenes
Sunset falls a little flat.
The dénouements of dawn release
Whole landscapes that will not survive
Catastrophe which intervenes
Between this interval and that.
What is the primaeval plot?
The rise and fall of consciousness
Within a given period.
The unity of time is not
Another bit of business
But an attribute of God.

Is that all it had to tell,
The world one thought so voluble
And interesting, is that all?
This formal, formulaic note
To Occupants who cannot spell
The seemingly insoluble
Conundrum of the capital
Letter kindly nature wrote
Whose illegibility
Prompts illiterate complaint.

Yet are the characters not fair
Despite their quaint asymmetry,
Manufactured, fresh as paint,
Inscrutable but plainly there?

A NOTE ABOUT THE AUTHOR

Daryl Hine was born in 1936 in British Columbia, Canada, and read Classics and Philosophy at McGill University, before going, with the aid of the first of several grants, to live in Paris. He came to this country in 1962, and in 1967 took a Ph.D. in Comparative Literature at the University of Chicago, where he has taught, as well as at Northwestern University and The University of Illinois (Chicago). From 1968 to 1978 he edited *Poetry* magazine. He has published ten earlier collections of verse, including a *Selected Poems*, and verse translations of *The Homeric Hymns*, and *Theocritus: Idylls and Epigrams*.

A NOTE ON THE TYPE

The text of this book is set in Linotype Garamond No. 3. It is not a true copy of any of the designs of Claude Garamond (1480–1561), but an adaptation of his types, which set the European standard for two centuries. It probably owes as much to the designs of Jean Jannon, a Protestant printer working in Sedan in the early seventeenth century, who had worked with Garamond's romans earlier, in Paris, and who was denied their use because of the Catholic censorship. Jannon's matrices came into the possession of the Imprimerie Nationale, where they were thought to be by Garamond himself, and so described when the Imprimerie revived the type in 1900. This particular version is based on an adaptation by Morris Fuller Benton.

Composition, printing and binding by
Heritage Printers, Charlotte, North Carolina.
Designed by Harry Ford